THE
HEART'S
COMPASS

NAVIGATING LOVE & RELATIONSHIPS
THROUGH TAROT

PUBLISHED BY RUBY JONES

Copyright© 2024 Ruby Jones
All rights reserved.
No part of this book may be reproduced, distributed, or transmitted in any form or by any means, including electronic, mechanical, photocopying, recording, or otherwise, without the prior written permission of the copyright owner. Brief quotations may be used in literary reviews and certain other non-commercial uses permitted by copyright law.
This book is a work of non-fiction. The information presented in this book is intended for educational purposes only. The author and publisher assume no responsibility for any errors or omissions in the material.

Published by Ruby Jones
Distributed by IngramSpark
For further information about this book and related works, visit www.lovetarotlounge.com

A SPECIAL NOTE OF GRATITUDE

Anne, for her loyalty, unwavering faith, and encouragement in acknowledging my gift.

Tanya, for the countless dinners and glasses of bubbles at her kitchen bench, allowing me to hone my craft.

Poppy, for the numerous readings where she patiently helped to unravel my love landscape. These hours allowed me to learn from one of the kindest and most insightful readers I have had the privilege to know.

with much love

Ruby Jones

TABLE OF CONTENTS

1	Introduction	06
2	Reading Rituals	22
3	Top 10 Love Cards	33
4	Love Cheat Sheets	58
5	Card Combinations	81
6	Bibliography	90
7	About the Author	91

INTRODUCTION

Hi there and welcome to my book. Get comfortable and settle in for an interesting read about the fascinating world of love tarot! Now, first things first. I've had many people ask me over the years how accurate tarot readings can be when predicting the most likely outcome for a particular situation. So, let's get this one out of the way because it's a good question, and I truly understand why some people are sceptical. However, I have personally found, and I'm certainly not the only one, that the tarot can be a powerful tool for gaining insight into our lives and all its tricky scenarios. With that out of the way, let me share my best explanation of how the tarot works with you.

Have you ever considered your life as a chessboard? As you know, each chess piece has a defined set of moves as they manoeuvre across the board. For example, the pawn piece can only move forward, never backward, and can capture one square on the diagonal. These moves a predictable. Now consider that each chess piece represents the people in our lives, and their movements reflect their probable habits and behaviours. Tarot readings can offer insights into the most likely outcome of a situation based on the anticipated movements and behaviours of those involved. Essentially, it's like a sneak preview into the future. Of course, if one of those 'pieces' in our life significantly deviates from their typical set of moves, it could impact the outcome. It's a unique way to view the tarot, don't you think? That's why a tarot reading can provide specific insights into our question based on the predictable actions of those involved at the time of the reading.

INTRODUCTION

A tarot reading can be complex and it can be challenging to understand what the cards are trying to convey, especially when there are so many possible card combinations. It can feel overwhelming at first, to unravel the narrative. Breaking down your questions can be helpful, and in my extensive tarot reading experience, there are three big life areas people are most curious about:

- Love Life
- Career
- Health*

With that tarot viewpoint in mind, I have crafted this book as a tool to help you navigate the most popular tarot topic – yes, you know it - the tricky world of love and relationships! With so much information available online and in books about the meanings of each tarot card, it can be a little daunting knowing where to start to answer these intriguing questions. This book draws on all that existing valuable knowledge available to provide you with a mini course in 'love tarot.' It's specifically geared towards answering your burning questions about love and relationships.

LOVE TAROT READING WORKSHOP

Remember these queries...

Keep in mind these common questions that people generally ask in regards to their love life:

- Will I meet someone special soon?
- Is there a future for myself and my current partner?
- Will I get back with my ex?
- Are there any signs that I will get married?
- Is my partner cheating on me?
- Will we ever have babies together?
- Does my partner really love me?
- Is my partner a good match for me?
- Is this true love?
- Are they in love with me?
- Is this just physical is it something more?
- Will I ever find my soul mate?

INTRODUCTION

HOW THIS BOOK WORKS

This book is designed as a resource for anyone interested in learning more about deciphering the tarot for love and relationship queries. I showcase the 10 big card players that are strong indicators of a love-focused reading. If the question is already about relationships, the appearance of any of these cards will be even more significant. I'll share The Love Cheat Sheet that is a handy tool for interpreting the meaning of the other cards in the context of love.

HOW THIS BOOK WORKS

Unfortunately, the tarot cannot give you the names and addresses of potential lovers! That would certainly be amazing! However, I have developed a rubric to help you piece their identity together. This section helps you classify the possible vocations and physical attributes of potential love interests or influencers in your relationship landscape. The Card Combos section is to help you pinpoint patterns and reveal love scenarios through your readings. And finally, the journal section is a brilliant way to keep track of your readings and reflect on them in your own words.

Using these tools will support you in unravelling your tarot love questions! Below outlines the best approach to honing your love tarot reading skills.

1. Familiarise yourself with the general card meanings and their love context.

2. Develop your reading ritual.

3. When you are about to commence your reading, shuffle your cards and focus on the querent and question.

4. Draw your cards and lay them out in your chosen spread configuration.

5. Refer to the top 10 cards, love cheat sheet, and people rubric to begin to weave your love interpretation for your question.

UPRIGHTS VERSUS REVERSALS

Tarot cards can be read with the upright and reverse meaning depending on how they fall during shuffling. I am like many tarot readers who choose not to incorporate reversals into their practice, preferring to focus solely on the upright meanings of the cards. This approach still allows for a comprehensive and insightful interpretation of the cards, as each card holds a wealth of symbolism and meaning in its upright position.

By only considering the upright meanings, you can still gain valuable insights into the questions and situations presented in a reading. The upright energy of the cards illuminates various aspects of the querent's life, offering guidance, clarity, and reflection on their current circumstances.

JOURNAL ACTIVITY

Write your own thoughties about using uprights versus reversals.

_____

_____

_____

_____

_____

SPREADS

There are numerous spreads you can use to apply to a love reading depending on your experience and knowledge. Popular spreads include the Astrology or Horoscope spread based on astrology's 12 houses of the zodiac, the 12-month spread, like the Horoscope spread, the Celtic Cross, 3-card, and 5-card spreads. However, for the purpose of this book, I have opted to keep it simple with a basic 3-card spread. As you progress and gain confidence, I suggest that you expand to a 5-card spread.

A helpful tip is to journal and document your spreads and card combinations. This will help you to draw out the story that the cards are trying to share with you and help build your confidence with your reading.

3 CARD SPREAD

The first spread we will cover is the 3-card spread. The 3-card spread is the simplest spread for answering any tarot question and in the context of love readings, this spread is no exception. The cards are place left to right.

1- Past: The first card is the Past card. This card signifies the past energy surrounding the question or what has taken place in the past.

2- Present: The second card is the Present. This card represents the current energy bounding the situation, essentially what is taking place at that time.

3- Future: The final card is Future. This card suggests the likely outcome for the question.

This is a great spread to help you become familiar with the various card combinations for love focused questions.

5 CARD SPREAD

The 5-card spread is next easiest spread just adding a little more complexity providing greater clarity for the question.

1- Past: This card is drawn first and signifies the past energy surrounding the question or what has taken place in the past.

2- Present: The next card drawn represents the current energy bounding the situation - what is taking place at that time.

3- Hidden influence: The third card drawn indicates the hidden aspects that might be affecting the situation that are not obvious or known.

4- Potential: This card represents what needs to be addressed based on the present and hidden influence cards. This card is often called the advice card.

5- Outcome. The final card suggests the most likely outcome should the querent heed the advice of the Potential card.

This spread is the next one I suggest you try once you are comfortable with the 3-card spread.

| past | present | hidden influence | potential / advice | outcome |

CELTIC CROSS

The Celtic Cross spread is steeped in tradition and is used broadly by many readers. It is somewhat more complex than the 3 and 5 card spreads. This spread offers a deep dive into your questions be it love or any other query.

There are 10 cards in this spread. Each card here is listed in order and placed in a cross configuration with a side column of 4 cards

1. The first card to lay down is the Cover or core card positioned in the centre. This card indicates the core of the question, the focus.

2. The next cards is placed across the cover card and represents what is crossing the situation. This card is what is directly impacting the situation for better or worse.

3. The card placed beneath these two is what is driving the situation. This card is the hidden energy that is driving or underpinning the situation.

4. The card positioned to the left of the central two is the influence from the past. This card indicates what has shaped the current situatio.

5. The card placed above the central two is the current influence over the situation. This card denotes the potential or advice to address any challenges surrounding the situation. It can also indicate an over-arching influence.

6. The card placed to the right is the near future: This card indicates what is coming up the querent in the near future.

7. We then place cards to the far right commencing at the bottom aligning to the third that you placed down. The first card in this column is The self-aspect: This card represents the querent's feelings about the situation.

8. Above this card is The home: This card represents your environment and those around the querent.

9. Another card is placed above representing The psychological aspect: This card represents hopes, dreams, fears or doubts of the querent.

10. The final card is the The outcome: This card suggest the likely outcome to the question.

> Additional cards can be drawn if clarification is needed after the outcome card.

LOVE TAROT READING WORKSHOP

The cards in the diagram that are shaded denotes the line of the home. These cards can be read left to right to give an indication of the overall environment of impacting the situation.

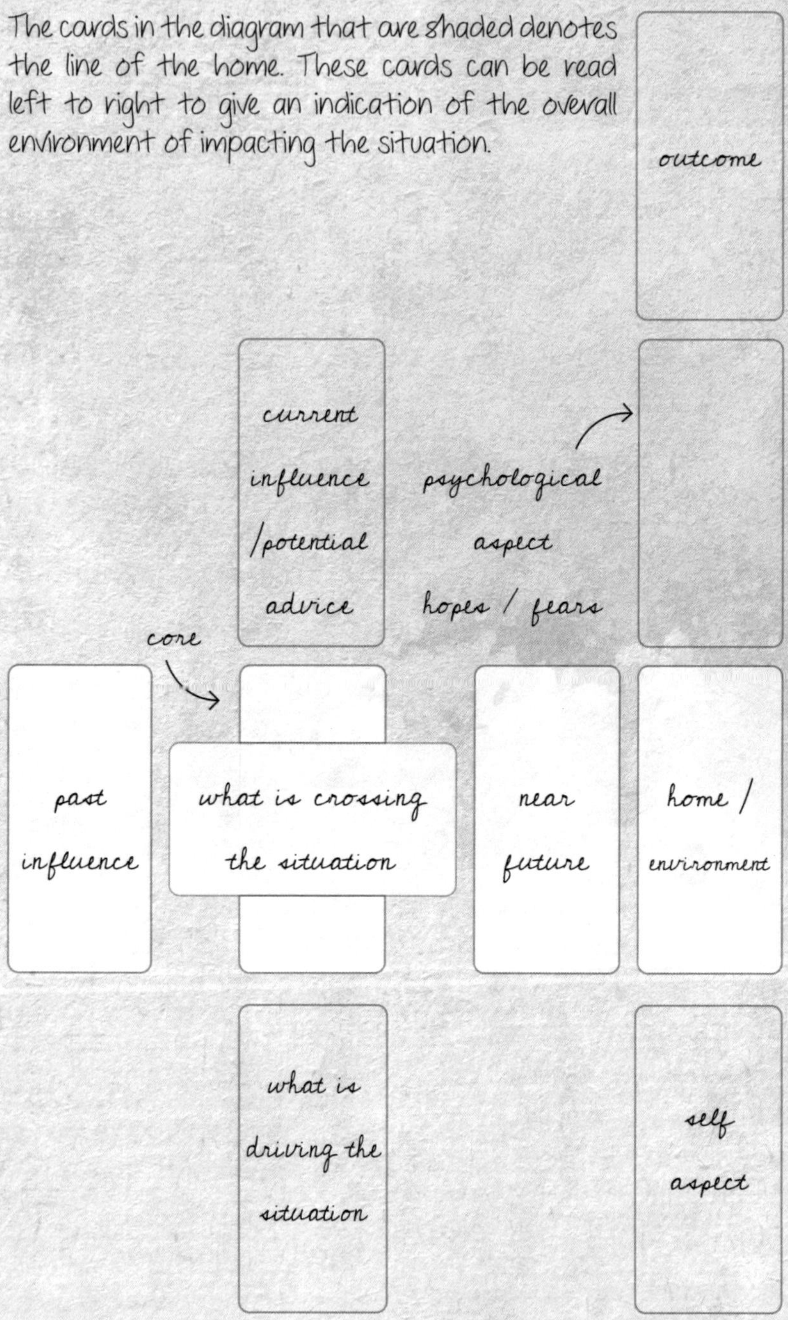

outcome

current influence / potential advice

psychological aspect hopes / fears

core →

past influence

what is crossing the situation

near future

home / environment

what is driving the situation

self aspect

HOW THIS BOOK WORKS

The art of reading tarot is to marry the card position in your chosen spread, such as the 5-card spread with the card meaning in the context of your question to create your love reading story. We will look at this in slightly more detail in the Card combination section of the course.

JOURNAL ACTIVITY

Use the space below to develop your own spread ideas for your love reading practice. Use the space on the opposite side to explain your card position and meaning

HOW THIS BOOK WORKS

Tarot readings are an energetic and interpretive practice that involves drawing on the querent's energy into the cards. Developing rituals or practices that facilitate this energetic transfer is an important part of your tarot reading. These small ceremonies can include burning candles, meditating, wafting sage sticks, and repeating mantras – experimenting to find the ones that resonate with you is part of your tarot reading journey.

You can shuffle the cards or have the querent shuffle and focus. It's important to store your cards in a way that resonates with you and follow a personal ritual that helps to create a robust and energetic connection between you and the querent.

Professional tarot readers often keep their cards in a specific box, wrapped in a silk scarf, or a small bag or pouch to protect their deck. They also follow a ritual or process before they begin reading to ensure that the energetic pathway is the strongest possible between themselves and the querent. This allows the deck to be imbued with the querent's energy which helps the cards reveal their story and provide the best insights.

Different readers use different preparatory techniques, such as meditation, repeating a mantra, or waving a shaman-style wand around themselves. There are no right or wrong approaches to preparing for a tarot reading. It's all about experimenting and finding the techniques that best connect with you. By exploring and investigating these different techniques, you can settle on the one you like best. Below are some rituals and practices that I use before I read.

STORING YOUR CARDS

I have an assortment of decks and select the one I want to use based on the vibe and connection I feel with the querant at the time. I store my current beloved deck in a leather pouch to protect it from physical damage along with a clear or rose quartz crystal. This is my little practice to keep the energy clean and clear and to help 'cleanse' the cards when they are not being used. The decks that I am not using get the VIP treatment and are stowed away in paisley silk scarves with crystals to keep them energetically safe and protect their positivity.

CLEARING SPRAYS

I have embraced the use of essential oils in my reading process. It's incredible how plants and herbs have been used for generations for their medicinal properties. Aromatherapy, which involves the use of botanical oils, is a powerful healing modality that can help not only physically but also emotionally and energetically. My own clearing spray recipe is a wonderful way to create a serene environment for you and your querent and ensure that the energetic pathways are clear. I encourage you to experiment with other combinations to create your own unique blend.

CLEARING SPRAY RECIPE

- 100ml spray bottle (not clear - amber, cobalt or black)
- Distilled water
- 30 drops of Geranium essential oil
- 20 drops of Sandalwood essential oil
- 30 drops of Frankincense essential oil
- 30 drops of Wild Orange (sweet) or Green Mandarin essential oil
- 20 drops of Tea Tree essential oil

Place all the oils into your spray bottle first then fill the bottle with distilled water. Mix well. Spray around you and the querent before you commence a reading.

DESIGNING YOUR OWN READING RITUAL

Designing your own reading ritual is a personal process. The practices that you embrace must resonate with you. There is no right or wrong; just right for you! I suggest experiencing other readers and observe their processes and practices to help inform your exploration. This will be truly valuable and inspirational. There is always something new to be learned from other readers either in their process or interpretation of the cards.

As for my own process, before I begin reading, I first spray around a little in between myself and the querent with my clearing spray - not on them! I like to take a few deep breaths, then close or divert my eyes to centre myself. I then ask the querent to shuffle the cards while focusing on their question or concern or if they prefer, I will shuffle. Once they have finished shuffling, I take the deck and lay out the cards in a specific pattern that I feel is appropriate for the reading. This process helps me create a clear, robust, and energetic connection between myself and the querent, and it leads to more accurate and meaningful readings.

I also offer my clients aromatherapy essential oil suggestions to emotionally and energetically overcome any roadblocks or healing that may arise in a reading. I have included my 'Aromatherapy Cheat Sheet' if you feel that is an area you would like to explore in your reading rituals.

Head to the journal section and note ideas to develop your own reading ritual - try them out and reflect on how you feel after trying them. Experiment with it and enjoy!

AROMATHERAPY CHEAT SHEET

Refer to the list below fo oils to support the following emotions. Experiement to see which ones blend together best.

EMOTION	SUGGESTED OILS
Fear	Neroli, Rose, Geranium, Jasmine & Sandalwood
Happiness	Lemon*, Lime*, Ylang Ylang, Peppermint** & Mandarin
Anger	Geranium & Roman Chamomile
Love	Rose, Magnolia, Frankincense, Geranium & Bergamot*
Sadness	Geranium, Ylang Ylang & Peppermint**
Letting go	Sandalwood & Lemongrass
Peace	Roman Chamomile, Patchouli, Lavender & Vetiver
Guilt	Bergamot*, LLitsea, Vetiver, Jasmine & Frankincense
Creativity	Davana & Wild Orange
Focus	Lemon*, Peppermint**, Magnolia, & Frankincense
Communication	Lavender
Intuition	Litsea, Sandalwood, Roman Chamomile & Rose
Stress	Tangerine*, Mandarin*, Lemon*, Peppermint**, Wild Orange*, Sandalwood, Ylang Ylang & Vetiver

CAUTION: Some essential oils should not be used during pregnancy, on babies or on children under 12 years of age. Check before use.
*Do not use before exposure to sunlight or apply neat to skin.
**Do not use before exposure to sunlight or apply neat to skin during pregnancy or on children under 7 years of age.

JOURNAL ACTIVITY

Use the space below to note your thoughts for your own reading ritual including your mantra thoughties!

Refer to the Aromatherapy Cheat Sheet for more oil ideas for sprays.

Experiment with your own love blend spray! Consider oils such as Rose, Helichrysm, Jasmine & Ylang Ylang

_____
_____
_____
_____
_____
_____
_____
_____

READING RITUALS

TIPS FOR TAROT READING

JUDGEMENT FREE ZONE

I believe it is important as a reader to keep an open mind and avoid bringing your preconceived notions to the reading. You are essentially mirroring the energy of the querent when you read, so if you bring along your own prejudices or judgements, then the reading will not necessarily be a true reflection of the situation, and may even block potential insights from coming through. Of course, you are certainly entitled to your own viewpoint on situations, however, I recommend not to bring them into the reading or be very clear when sharing your thoughts; stating clearly that these are your thoughts and not the cards. This for me, represents the utmost integrity of a reader.

WORK WITH YOUR INTUITION

The cards are merely a tool to interpret your intuition and the energy of the querent. If something does not feel right, take another look - that's okay! Sometimes the cards want to give you other story elements that might inform your primary question and that can be tricky to decipher. So, looking at the cards again or asking the question a little differently can sometimes help you to tweeze out the messages being shared.

LISTEN

You may have heard the term 'speak in the direct ratio of your ears to your mouth.' It means, listening twice as much as you speak! Quite often querents are seeking to be heard as well as seeking answers to their questions. That in itself can be immensely healing and insightful for them. Listen to your querent with an open mind and heart because your time and generosity can be invaluable to the other person.

SHARE WHAT YOU SEE

Be honest! I know the other person on the other side of the table may desperately want to hear something in particular, however, it is important to share exactly what you see, for that is the message that needs to be shared. We often do not like what we hear but sometimes it is what we need to hear in order to grow, move forward, or make vital choices.

LOVE TAROT READING WORKSHOP

Love is a hot topic when it comes to tarot readings! I've showcased the top 10 big-shot cards that scream "love and relationships" when they appear in a reading. If one or more of these cards makes an appearance, especially if you're being asked about love and relationships specifically, it's significant. The cards convey, "Love is in the air."

The Love Cheat Sheet is so handy because you can use it to piece together the love narratives the cards are trying to communicate to you, especially when other cards show up that might not seem directly related to the topic of love at first glance. This cheat sheet is your secret weapon for getting to the heart of the matter.

Don't forget to use the journal section to jot down the cards you pull and what you think they're telling you. This journalling is a game-changer for boosting your confidence and getting a deeper understanding of how love is playing out in the readings. Whether you're a tarot beginner or you've been dabbling for a while, tracking your readings like this can really help you see the patterns and get clearer messages from the cards.

As mentioned previously, there is a plethora of information available on the meanings of each card - I strongly encourage you to explore and define your own interpretations so that you connect to your tarot practice to craft your own love chronicles and use this book as a catalyst for this study.

THE LOVERS

The Lovers card, associated with Gemini and the number 6 symbolises romantic partnerships - it's a complex tapestry of energies and choices. While it does signify love and union, it also represents the interplay of opposing forces, like yin and yang, or masculine and feminine energies. This card appears when one is faced with significant decisions, similar to standing at a crossroads and pondering the right path forward.

Phrases to keep in mind:
- Love and marriage
- Soul mate connections
- Intense passion and attraction
- Deep intimacy
- Life-altering decisions.

FOR THE SINGLE FOLK:

The Lovers card is hinting at a new romantic chapter—this could be a brand-new sweetheart or the rekindling of an old flame. There's a bit of an air of choice with this one, however. If the Lovers appears, it's giving you a heads-up to think things through, especially if you're juggling more than one potential love interest!

FOR THOSE ALREADY COUPLED UP:

It's as if The Lovers are waving a flag signalling that an aspect of your relationship that needs your TLC. It's all about weighing up what's happening in your partnership and understanding the impact of any decisions you're about to make.

In essence, The Lovers serves as your guiding beacon in the love landscape, advising you to proceed with caution and mindfulness. It encourages thoughtful consideration before taking any leaps, particularly when matters of the heart are at stake.

JOURNAL ACTIVITY

Write your own thoughties about The Lovers.

_____

_____

_____

_____

_____

_____

_____

THE HIEROPHANT

The Hierophant is like the wise teacher of the tarot deck. It's all about adhering to traditions, moral values, and spiritual growth. This card is astrologically associated with Taurus and the number 5 and appears when it's time to plunge into learning, gaining wisdom, and even sitting at the feet of a mentor or spiritual guide. This card is giving you the hint that connecting with something bigger—like diving into your religious roots or exploring a belief system that calls to you — are potentially on the agenda.

When the Hierophant makes an appearance, think traditional ceremonies and community vibes, like weddings or other meaningful gatherings that tie you to others through shared beliefs and practices. It's all about embracing and respecting the rules and rituals that have stood the test of time.

PHRASES TO KEEP IN MIND:

- Sticking to traditional paths
- Rituals and ceremonies
- Seeking or offering spiritual guidance
- Finding a mentor or becoming one

- Following the rules
- Belief in faith
- Being part of structured groups or communities.

In love readings, the Hierophant is a positive sign, indicating things are moving in a positive, traditional direction.

FOR THE SINGLE FOLK:

This card is your cue that going the traditional route in your love life might just be the winning strategy. Think old-school romance, where shared values and beliefs light the way to finding that special someone who really gets you.

FOR THOSE ALREADY COUPLED UP:

The Hierophant's presence suggests your partnership could be heading towards a more traditional commitment—yes, even marriage. But it also nudges you to consider your partner's beliefs and how embracing or understanding them more could bring you closer.

In essence, the Hierophant is about finding depth and meaning in our connections, guided by the wisdom of traditions and the shared journey towards spiritual growth.

JOURNAL ACTIVITY

Write your own thoughties about The Hierophant.

_____

_____

_____

THE EMPRESS

The Empress is a beacon of feminine power! She radiates fertility, sensuality, and nurturing energy. It is no surprise that this card is astrologically associated with Venus and the number 3. She's the ultimate symbol of motherhood, representing abundance, love, and the cosy warmth of home. When the Empress appears, it's your cue to tap into your feminine side, embracing your passions, emotions, intuition, and creativity with open arms. That goes for the men too!

This card isn't merely about motherhood in the literal sense - it's about birthing new ideas, projects, and relationships. It's all about that fertile energy, where creativity blooms, new life sprouts, and love flows freely. So, whether you're looking to start a family, launch a new business venture, or simply infuse your life with more love and abundance, the Empress is a wonderful card to see appear.

PHRASES TO KEEP IN MIND:

- Pregnancy and maternal instincts
- Unleashing your creativity
- Getting in touch with your sensual side

- Abundance in all its forms
- Building a strong, loving relationship
- Finding joy and contentment in the little things.

The Empress energy feels like a warm embrace from the universe, reminding you to nurture yourself and others, follow your passions, and revel in the beauty and abundance of life.

When it comes to love readings, The Empress is like hitting the jackpot. This card packs a joyful punch, signalling not just romance, but the potential for growth, abundance, and even pregnancy. The universe is saying, "Love is about to blossom."

FOR THE SINGLE FOLK:

The Empress is your green light for love. It's a sign that a true, deep connection might be just around the corner. But here's the kicker—even if you're not actively seeking it, love could still come knocking at your door. The energy of The Empress is powerful.

FOR THOSE ALREADY COUPLED UP:

Get ready for some serious heart-to-heart moments. The Empress is all about deepening your connection with your partner, and bringing more authenticity and love into your relationship. If starting a family is on your mind, this card calls for you to go for it! Even if pregnancy is not on your agenda, expect major positive shifts in your relationship. (NB: The Empress does not indicate pregnancy on its own, other cards are required to strongly indicate pregnancy such as Page of Cups and 3 of Cups.)

In essence, when The Empress appears in a love reading, it's the universe enlightening you that love is abundant and ready to bloom in your life.

JOURNAL ACTIVITY

Write your own thoughties about The Empress.

_____
_____
_____
_____
_____
_____
_____
_____
_____
_____
_____

ACE OF CUPS

The appearance of the Ace of Cups indicates the stirrings of the heart and those unmistakable butterflies fluttering in your stomach. Oh, what a lovely feeling! It's all about embarking on new emotional journeys—be it a budding romance, the deepening of a friendship, or a connection that could very well end up being "The One."

PHRASES TO KEEP IN MIND:

- Thrilling tender feelings
- Warmth of friendship
- Excitement of a new romantic adventure
- Sweet surprise of an old flame rekindling
- Rush of new, loving emotions
- Falling madly in love
- Joy of childbirth
- Sensitivity and kindness.

FOR THE SINGLE FOLK:

Get ready to celebrate! A new love interest might be around the corner, or perhaps an old flame is making a comeback. Look out for heartfelt messages or gestures from a beloved someone. The Ace of Cups is the promise of fresh, exciting love feelings that are heading your way.

FOR THOSE ALREADY COUPLED UP:

Feeling like things have been a bit stagnant? The Ace of Cups is a sign of emotional rejuvenation. It's time to reignite those flames of love, reminding you why you fell for each other in the first place. This card is your green light for renewal and deepening the emotional bonds that have felt a bit frayed around the edges.

In essence, the Ace of Cups is about opening your heart to the possibilities of love and connection, offering a chance to start anew with a clean emotional slate. Whether you're single or happily taken, this card heralds a period of emotional growth, happiness, and the nurturing of relationships that matter most.

JOURNAL ACTIVITY

Write your own thoughties about Ace of Cups.

_____

_____

_____

_____

_____

_____

_____

LOVE TAROT READING WORKSHOP

TWO OF CUPS

The Two of Cups is like a cosmic bow to the beauty of harmonious relationships. When this card appears, it's highlighting the deep, meaningful connections that are founded in friendship but have the potential to bloom into something even more beautiful and romantic. Think of it as the universe's way of saying, "There's something special here." If you have been parted from a beloved, the Two of Cups can indicate that reunions and reconciliations may be on the cards, literally!

PHRASES TO KEEP IN MIND:

- A magnetic attraction
- The start or deepening of a love affair
- The foundation of friendship turning into a partnership
- The dance of union
- The possibility of marriage on the horizon
- A pledge of commitment
- The beauty of balance and equilibrium.

FOR THE SINGLE FOLK:

The Two of Cups suggests that love might be closer than you

think, potentially with someone you already know well. This emerging relationship promises to be one where you see eye to eye, meeting each other as equals on this journey of love.from a beloved someone.

FOR THOSE ALREADY COUPLED UP:

This card is a wonderful omen, suggesting your partnership is moving towards a deeper commitment such as marriage. It celebrates mutual respect and admiration and serves as a reminder that maintaining this beautiful balance requires both effort and dedication.

In essence, the Two of Cups is all about the magic that happens when two people come together in understanding, respect, and love. Whether you're single and hoping for love or already in a partnership that's moving towards greater commitment, this card symbolises deep and fulfilling connection.this card heralds a period of emotional growth, happiness, and the nurturing of relationships that matter most.

JOURNAL ACTIVITY

Write your own thoughties about Two of Cups.

_____

_____

_____

_____

_____

TEN OF CUPS

The Ten of Cups is the universe throwing a party in your honour, where everything is about happiness, love, and the kind of joy that fills up your whole heart. Picture the perfect day where the sun is shining, the birds are singing, and everything feels just right. That's the vibe of this card, especially when it comes to matters of the heart.

PHRASES TO KEEP IN MIND:

- Celebrating love with a joyful wedding
- Friendships that are real and authentic
- A family life filled with laughter and love
- Unity that feels natural, and founded in deep trust
- A rapport that makes every conversation bliss
- Spiritual happiness that lights up your soul.

FOR THE SINGLE FOLK:

The Ten of Cups signals that the universe is about to spice up your love life in the most wonderful way. Expect to meet someone with whom you share not just an attraction, but deep, foundational beliefs and a sense of unity and security.

FOR THOSE ALREADY COUPLED UP:

If you're already in a relationship with someone, this card is a beautiful sign that your relationship is about to level up to the kind of contentment and happiness that most people dream about. Challenges seem to melt away, leaving in their place a deep, secure contentment and joy that comes from true partnership and shared dreams.

In essence, the Ten of Cups is a reminder that joy, love, and happiness are not just possible, they're on the horizon. Whether you're single and hoping for a meaningful connection or in a relationship and looking forward to deepening your bond, this card is a bright, shining light guiding you toward emotional fulfilment and bliss.

JOURNAL ACTIVITY

Write your own thoughties about Ten of Cups.

_____

_____

_____

_____

_____

FOUR OF WANDS

The suit of Wands is all about our energy, that life force, and what innately drives us. The Four of Wands is like throwing a party after a marathon of hard work, enjoying each moment of celebration and well-deserved rest. It marks the joy of reaching a milestone that once seemed distant, urging you to pause, appreciate the journey, and revel in your achievements. This card is all about building something lasting, whether it's laying the bricks for a home, fortifying the bonds of a relationship, or anchoring yourself in a community that uplifts you.

PHRASES TO KEEP IN MIND:

- A well-earned rest basking in the fruits of your labour
- The warmth and stability of a happy, secure home
- The beginning of a long term, committed relationship filled with promise
- A time of prosperity and creative fulfillment
- The excitement of romantic possibilities and celebrations.

FOR THE SINGLE FOLK:

This card brings a message of potential and promise. A new

love interest sees not just the person you are today but the incredible future you could build together. They're in it for the long haul, eager to explore how your relationship can grow and flourish.

FOR THOSE ALREADY COUPLED UP:

The Four of Wands confirms that your relationship is on solid ground. Your partner feels deeply connected and satisfied with the harmony you share. If you're anticipating taking things to the next level, this card is a reassuring sign that those commitments are on the horizon, and your partner is just as excited about the idea of celebrating your future together as you are.

In essence, the Four of Wands invites you to take a moment to celebrate where you are right now, acknowledging the journey that brought you here and the foundations you've built. It's a reminder that achievements, both personal and shared, deserve recognition and celebration, setting the stage for the next chapter of your journey with a heart full of joy and anticipation.

JOURNAL ACTIVITY

Write your own thoughties about Four of Wands.

_____

_____

_____

_____

TEN OF PENTACLES

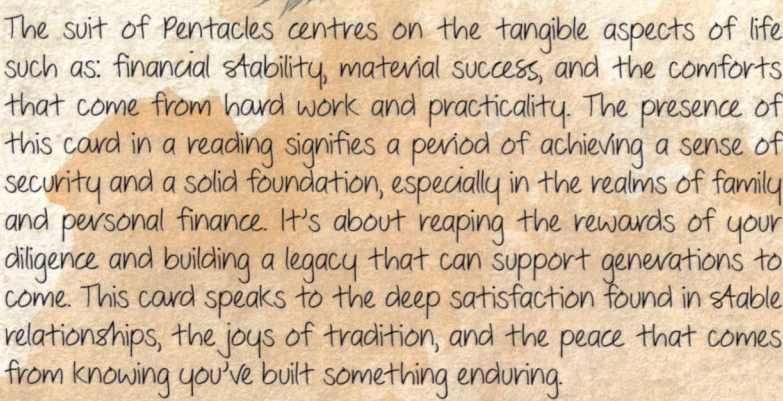

The suit of Pentacles centres on the tangible aspects of life such as: financial stability, material success, and the comforts that come from hard work and practicality. The presence of this card in a reading signifies a period of achieving a sense of security and a solid foundation, especially in the realms of family and personal finance. It's about reaping the rewards of your diligence and building a legacy that can support generations to come. This card speaks to the deep satisfaction found in stable relationships, the joys of tradition, and the peace that comes from knowing you've built something enduring.

PHRASES TO KEEP IN MIND:

- The warmth and security of strong family foundations

- Achieving stability and material success

- Celebratory events like weddings and births and marking new beginnings and unions

- Building unions that also make sense financially, reflecting shared values and practicality.

- The importance of legacy, tradition, and long-term commitment.

FOR THE SINGLE FOLK:

This card suggests that anyone entering your life now sees your relationship as more than just a fleeting connection. They're playing the long game, where emotional bonds are enriched by shared goals, values, and a practical approach to life. While the whirlwind of romance might not be at the forefront, there's a promise of stability and a future where both of you can prosper.

FOR THOSE ALREADY COUPLED UP:

This card underscores a period of contentment and mutual satisfaction in your partnership. It suggests that you're both on the same wavelength, valuing compatibility, security, and the idea of building something lasting together. The support from friends and family further cements the sense that this relationship is meant to be, possibly indicating that it's time to consider formalising your commitment to each other if you haven't already. Exciting!

In essence, this card is a reminder that while love and relationships encompass the emotional and spiritual, they also thrive on practicality and stability. The achievements and security you've built—or are in the process of building—are not just for the here and now but for the future you envision together.

JOURNAL ACTIVITY

Write your own thoughties about Four of Wands.

_____

_____

_____

ACE OF WANDS

Inspiration, new opportunities, and growth underpin the Ace of Wands. This card is strongly associated with physical chemistry and the male phallic symbol. In the realm of love, the Ace of Wands is telling you to brace yourself for some seriously exciting love feelings! The universe has flicked on the green light to encourage you forth and embrace the new love opportunity before you. This card is bursting with that 'new adventure' energy — imagine sparks flying, hearts racing, and copious butterfly feelings

PHRASES TO KEEP IN MIND:

- Sizzling chemistry
- Diving into something new
- Feeling hopeful and filled with enthusiasm
- Doors thrust open
- Fresh ideas and emotions
- Feeling driven and laser-focused
- Sparks of inspiration.

FOR THE SINGLE FOLK:

Your love life's about to get a major adrenaline shot! Whether you've caught someone's eye or you're just feeling those first date butterflies, it's all about feeling that rush, being totally smitten, and seeing love through an optimistic lens.

FOR THOSE ALREADY COUPLED UP:

If you've been craving a little reminder that the passion is alive and kicking, this card appears to remind you that there is still a spark between you both. That there is still plenty of fire. It's less about long heart-to-hearts and more about those, "You still make my heart skip a beat" moments.

In essence, whether you're single and ready to mingle or already with your special someone, the Ace of Wands is about embracing those fresh, exhilarating feelings and letting them lead you on your love adventure and see where it takes you.

JOURNAL ACTIVITY

Write your own thoughties about Ace of Wands.

_____
_____
_____
_____
_____
_____
_____

OTHER CARDS TO NOTE

The Sun, The Devil, and the Page of Cups are significant in love readings; however, they don't exclusively signify that the reading is solely about love. When combined with other cars these cards add depth and insight to love-related questions. Let's delve deeper into their significance:

THE SUN

The Sun is an all-round positive card in any context, not merely love. In love readings, The Sun represents a period of deep connection, happiness, and harmony between partners. It signifies warmth, vitality, and mutual understanding in the relationship. This card encourages embracing love with confidence and openness, signalling a thriving and fulfilling romantic connection.

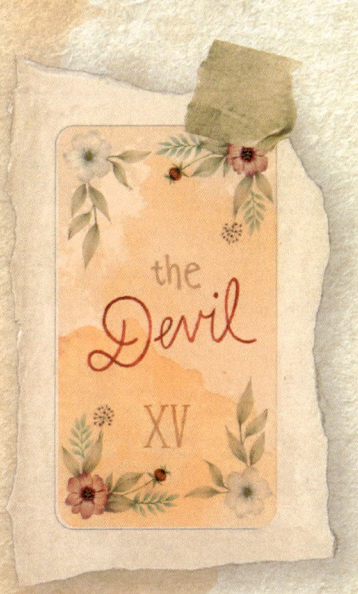

THE DEVIL

The Devil in a love reading is traditionally thought to highlight conflicts, toxic behaviours, or co-dependent dynamics within the relationship. It urges honesty, transparency, and the courage to address underlying issues. However, it is important to note, in a positive context, the Devil card indicates a binding commitment, especially when paired with other positive love cards.

PAGE OF CUPS

The Page of Cups signifies the emergence of new feelings, romantic gestures, or emotional messages between partners. It encourages vulnerability, authenticity, and deeper emotional connections. This card reminds individuals to listen to their intuition and nurture the romantic spark in their relationship.

LOVE TAROT READING WORKSHOP

NO SWORDS - WHY?

As for Sword cards, while they typically denote conflict and focus on thoughts rather than emotions, their presence will still impact the narrative of a love reading. They may highlight challenges or obstacles that need to be overcome in the relationship, providing valuable insights into communication issues or mental barriers. However, their appearance doesn't necessarily indicate that the reading is exclusively about love and relationships and that is why they are not included above top 10.

TOP 10 LOVE CARDS

LOVE TAROT READING WORKSHOP

LOVE CHEAT SHEETS

The Love Cheat Sheet is a valuable tool to understand the implications of tarot cards in the context of love and relationships. These cards punctuate the love narratives adding the important details to the significant love cards.

In the love and relationships landscape, the Minor Arcana offers nuanced insights into the everyday dynamics and emotional undercurrents that shape our connections. Each suit—Cups, Wands, Pentacles, and Swords—highlights different aspects of relationships, from emotional bonds and passion to practical matters and communication challenges. Here's how each suit of the Minor Arcana can be interpreted in a love context.

MINOR ARCANA

CUPS — EMOTIONS AND RELATIONSHIPS

Ace of Cups* — A joyous card signifying a new beginning in love. This is a very positive card that indicates true, unconditional love, emotional fulfillment and spiritual union not merely based on physical attraction.

Two of Cups* — Epitomises a partnership developing between two people based on mutual values, respect, and appreciation for one another. This card represents a promising physical and emotional soul connection and can signify a marriage proposal or engagement.

Three of Cups — A card of celebrations, weddings, engagements, anniversaries, baby showers, and reunions. The mood of this card is fun, excitement, and positivity. This is a card of kinship, comradery, and friendship — lovers and friends.

Four of Cups — A tendency to be self-absorbed and reflect on the deficiencies in your relationship is indicated by the appearance of this card. Apathy, despondency, boredom, and indifference is the energy of this card indicating the need for gratitude in your relationship.

Five of Cups — The feeling of loss, disappointment, and regret in a relationship is the key message of this card. It also signifies that all hope is not lost, and this experience will open more possibilities and new opportunities in time.

Six of Cups — This card is about familiarity, past connections, family, and children. It indicates a soul connection, or that someone that you know or someone from your childhood is your new romantic interest on the horizon.

Seven of Cups	Romantic choices and indecision are the key messages of this card. The appearance of this card indicates that you have romantic options before you. It is a card of illusions and having one's head in the clouds romantically.
Eight of Cups	The realisation that aspects of your relationship no longer serve you and there is a need to walk away and let go. Extracting yourself from this situation is a positive move as you are moving towards a better romantic state of being.
Nine of Cups	A card of wishes and fulfillment. This is a very positive card in a relationship reading and signifies that your romantic desires will be fulfilled.
Ten of Cups*	Harmony, joy, fulfillment, and family values are the key messages of this card. This card suggests long-term happiness and a deep and harmonious connection in a romantic relationship. It can also indicate starting a family.
Page of Cups	A card of loving messages, dreamy, romantic, and idealistic love. Your romantic interest loves you, however they may be a little emotionally immature. It is a very encouraging card in a love reading.
Knight of Cups*	This card indicates a love returning to your life. It is another card of intense romance, proposals, offers, and good news. This card signifies a gentle charming young man who is affectionate and warm.
Queen of Cups	Warmth, compassion, nurturing, and understanding is the essence of this card. It indicates a love that is harmonious, genuine, and from a supportive place. The queen is intuitive and suggests a spiritual connection.
King of Cups	A devoted and balanced lover founded in wisdom and diplomacy. He strikes a balance between emotions and intellect. He is the evolution from the less mature, Knight of Cups.

LOVE TAROT READING WORKSHOP

WANDS — CREATIVITY AND INSPIRATION

Ace of Wands
A card of intensity signifying a passionate new beginning. A positive card in a love reading indicates mutual physical attraction, flirtation, sensuality, and strong chemistry.

Two of Wands
Partnership and choice are the energies surrounding this card. This card indicates a choice between two pathways. It is a card of planning the relationship and looking ahead into future.

Three of Wands
Expansion, growth, and optimism. Your prospective love interest or current one views your relationship with potential. There is momentum here to move forward together.

Four of Wands*
A card of celebrations, family, and home. This is a significant card in a love reading indicating that celebrations such as weddings are on the horizon. This card indicates there is trust and security in this relationship.

Five of Wands
Conflict, completion, and tension embody this card. There is conflict with another or within yourself around a relationship situation. This card calls you to assess how you handle this conflict – with aggression or kindness.

Six of Wands
Success, achievement, and victory in a relationship or love situation. This card is about solidarity – you or your romantic interest are intensely proud to have each other in their lives, or you will triumph in your romantic life.

Seven of Wands
Defending your position and standing up for yourself may be necessary in your romantic world. This card can indicate your romantic interest in being willing to defend you and your relationship if your relationship has experienced judgement, or criticism from others.

Eight of Wands	There is a significant pace associated with this card. This card often indicates 'love at first sight', immediate chemistry, or 'Cupid's arrows' launching into the air. There is a relationship incoming at a speed along with a lot of communication.
Nine of Wands	Perseverance is the essence of this card. Previous experiences have placed you or your love interest on guard and you are cautious. However, you are both prepared to work through any differences and make the relationship work.
Ten of Wands	Overwhelm and burden are the energies of this card. You or your love interest are currently feeling drained and worried. This emotional state is distracting either or both of you from focusing on your relationship, or aspects of your relationship are burdensome and heavy.
Page of Wands	Passionate and intense messages characterise this card. There is excitement and adventure surrounding the energy of this card signifying an energetic relationship.
Knight of Wands	There is a mutual attraction between you and your love interest founded on a love of the challenge and the chase. There is speedy development with this connection.
Queen of Wands	There is an optimistic, confident, and cheerful energy with the appearance of this card encouraging you to draw out these aspects in yourself within the relationship. This connection is vibrant, vivacious, and warm founded on a generous spirit.
King of Wands	A motivated, loyal, and charming lover with a passion for excitement and the thrill of a challenge. Expect a sexual adventure with the appearance of this card.

PENTACLES — MATERIAL WORLD AND STABILITY

Ace of Pentacles
This card announces financial new beginnings or a significant monetary influx. It reflects a relationship based on generosity, loyalty, and practicality, promising prosperity, and stability in this new connection.

Two of Pentacles
The need to find balance and harmony characterises this card, urging flexibility to achieve romantic equilibrium. It suggests that the energy in the relationship may fluctuate and calls for careful consideration.

Three of Pentacles
Symbolising teamwork and collaboration, this card highlights the importance of working together towards shared physical or tangible objectives beyond emotional goals, fostering practical growth together.

Four of Pentacles
Cautioning against prioritising material gain over emotional needs, this card also indicates a desire to maintain the connection. It underscores the tendency to cling to both physical possessions and emotional attachments.

Five of Pentacles
Loss and sadness permeate this card, suggesting feelings of loss or sadness regarding aspects of the relationship that have diminished over time, prompting some reflection on what has been lost.

Six of Pentacles
Generosity and charity are central themes here, emphasising the need for reciprocity in fostering a healthy, fulfilling relationship. It hints at assistance from others in relationship endeavours.

Seven of Pentacles
Reflecting on relationship efforts, this card indicates reaping the rewards and growth within the relationship. It prompts reflection and reassessment of romantic achievements, signalling growth and fruition.

Eight of Pentacles	Representing diligence and effort, this card suggests that work is required for the relationship to thrive. It underscores the necessity of labour and dedication in nurturing love or potential connections.
Nine of Pentacles	A card of luxury, success, and independence, it indicates a relationship where both individuals thrive on each other's individuality. It suggests a successful and independent partner.
Ten of Pentacles*	Long-term stability and building family legacies are the major energies of this card. This card signifies happiness and contentment based on shared family values with a practical approach to establishing financial security.
Page of Pentacles	This card embodies studiousness and diligence, suggesting that a similar approach is needed in your relationship. There's an aura of steadiness and consistency surrounding this card, advocating for a thoughtful and committed mindset.
Knight of Pentacles	Lacking in speed, this card represents a methodical and slow-moving progress. While an offer may come forth, it will be stable and steady, grounded in loyalty. However, expect a pace that is deliberate rather than swift.
Queen of Pentacles	Nurturing and practical, this card exudes an energy grounded in financial prowess. With a mother-earth demeanour, the Queen of Pentacles possesses innate sensuality and warmth, coupled with a strong sense of compassion.
King of Pentacles	A materially resourceful and generous lover, the King of Pentacles offers stability and commitment. Serious and preferring security, this king approaches relationships with maturity, embracing a slow and steady approach.

SWORDS	THOUGHTS AND COMMUNICATION
Ace of Swords	New beginnings and truthful communication are central to this card. Share your feelings openly and honestly with your partner or potential partner.
Two of Swords	Difficult decisions, stalemates and being in denial are the key energies of this card. It also indicates that someone is finding vulnerability challenging requiring them to connect with their emotions.
Three of Swords	Heartbreak, sorrow, grief, and separation are the primary themes of this card. It indicates that this relationship is struggling with an element of karmic energy surrounding the connection.
Four of Swords	This is a card of respite and the need to pause. There may be a necessity to heal from a previous relationship and find peace. Self-care is required so that you can replenish yourself in order to give to others.
Five of Swords	Potential hostilities surround this card. Conflict is part of relationships however this also implies ill intent behind the conflict. Ensure that you or your partner are not manipulating the situation.
Six of Swords	This card signifies that the relationship is improving and moving into smoother waters. This card indicates a long-distance relationship or communicating or meeting in an online environment.
Seven of Swords	This card represents deceit, lack of transparency, lies or potential betrayal (not necessarily infidelity). It also indicates emotional unavailability or distance for self-preservation, or the need for boundaries.

Eight of Swords	This card indicates restriction or feeling trapped and helpless in a romantic situation. It represents self-imposed limitations and being unable to see the way forward out of a predicament. Know there are choices to change the situation.
Nine of Swords	A relationship may be causing anxiety and fear. This card indicates the need to reflect on the cause of the anxiety and possibly take time to address the trigger. Healing may be required before moving forward.
Ten of Swords	A romantic situation is no longer tenable and signifies that change is on the horizon. There is an air of betrayal or sadness with this inevitable change. Endings open the opportunity for new beginnings.
Page of Swords	This connection is mentally stimulating based on integrity and authenticity. There is an aspect of immaturity with this card. The relationship may not be long-term; however, it is rooted in honest communication about the situation.
Knight of Swords	A card of harsh, direct communication, as well as representing impatience and daring. This card signifies a relationship based on mental intellect rather than emotion, sharing mutual values, and perspectives on current affairs.
Queen of Swords	Not the most romantic card however this signifies forthrightness, honesty, loyalty, and pragmaticism. The energy of this card indicates emotional coldness and distance; however, she embodies intelligence and humour.
King of Swords	This card symbolises unobtrusive loyalty, honesty, trust, and rationality. Your partner or potential partner thrives on intellectual conversation and open and honest communication. It is a mature relationship that is more cerebral than physical.

MAJOR ARCANA

Each Major Arcana card can reflect significant themes in love, from the Fool's new beginnings to the World's completion of a cycle. When these cards appear, they can indicate overarching lessons or major influences affecting the relationship. Additionally, some readers interpret certain Major Arcana cards as representing people in a love context, adding another layer of insight into the dynamics at play.

This Cheat Sheet offers a focused lens through which to view the myriad possibilities of love and relationships as reflected in the tarot, making it an indispensable tool for those seeking guidance in matters of the heart.

CARD	LOVE CONTEXT
Fool	Exuding youthful, naive, and exuberant energy, it suggests new beginnings or a fresh approach. It signifies the early stages of romance or an immature approach to matters of the heart.
The Magician	This card embodies potential, where endless possibilities abound. It signifies dreams manifesting into reality, mastery, and, occasionally, manipulation in its negative aspect. It denotes virility and of possessing the talents needed to instigate change. In romantic relationships, communication and connections are robust and profound.
The High Priestess	This card delves into the subconscious and all that is secretive and concealed within. In the realm of relationships, it signifies a soulful and intuitive connection or a clandestine bond that is not openly acknowledged.
The Empress*	A relationship abundant in harmony, sensuality, and healing, the Empress often indicates the potential for marriage, pregnancy, or childbirth, signifying a deeply fulfilling and fertile connection.

LOVE CHEAT SHEETS

CARD	LOVE CONTEXT
The Emperor	Epitomising authority, leadership, power, and exuding an aura of supreme control, the Emperor in love may suggest the presence of a protective individual, offering a sense of stability and security. However, in a negative light, it could signify excessively controlling behaviour or the abuse of power.
The Hierophant*	This card embodies convention and constancy. In romantic contexts, it signifies a traditional approach to unions, emphasising loyalty and devotion.
The Lovers*	This card holds great significance in love and relationships. It places love at the forefront and suggests that important choices lie ahead regarding romantic connections or other significant life matters.
The Chariot	Radiating forward motion, this card signifies progress toward a victorious romantic outcome with momentum following a period of balancing opposing forces and overcoming obstacles.
Strength	Strength projects physicality and potency. When paired with certain cards, it can suggest passionate sexual encounters. Moreover, it symbolises remarkable stability within a relationship, portraying your bond as a formidable force to be reckoned with.
The Hermit	This card signifies introspection, hinting at past life or soul connections, or the return of someone from your past. There's a deep sense of knowing and familiarity attached to it. Additionally, it suggests the necessity of healing emotional wounds stemming from past disappointments.
Wheel of Fortune	With the appearance of this card, luck or fortune is generally shifting for the better. Your romantic landscape is undergoing change, potentially indicating the meeting of a love interest during travel.

CARD	LOVE CONTEXT
Wheel of Fortune	With the appearance of this card, luck or fortune is generally shifting for the better. Your romantic landscape is undergoing change, potentially indicating the meeting of a love interest during travel.
Justice	Balance is the central energy of this card, emphasising cerebral rather than emotional evaluation in romantic matters, urging for equilibrium. Caution against getting carried away is advised.
The Hanged Man	This card symbolises a state of suspension where progress is either slow or temporarily stalled. In romantic matters, this limbo state typically occurs when feelings have developed but further progression is needed. It also suggests the importance of reassessing romantic affairs with a fresh perspective and approaching them in a different manner.
Death	The emergence of this card often triggers fear, but it signals imminent transformation and upheaval in the current situation. While the changes may not always be welcomed, these are deemed necessary.
Temperance	This card emphasises moderation, harmony, and patience, offering a message of healing and tranquillity. It may also suggest meaningful connections with individuals from diverse ethnic backgrounds.
The Devil	This card warns of overindulgence and of poor self-control, pointing to behaviours that may spiral into substance abuse, co-dependency, or attempts to dominate. However, in a brighter light and with affirmation from accompanying cards, it could also symbolise a deep, binding commitment, offering a glimmer of positivity amidst cautionary tales.

CARD	LOVE CONTEXT
Tower	This card signals a profound change, signalling the breakdown of established patterns in your life. It could reveal the surprising entrance of a new love interest, catching you completely off guard, or the unexpected unravelling of a current romantic scenario, steering your heart's journey towards uncharted territories.
The Star	This card overflows with optimism and hope, urging you to embrace a positive outlook in your romantic endeavours. It encourages you to cultivate spiritual contentment and embrace renewal, promising a brighter path ahead in matters of the heart.
The Moon	This card is steeped in the energies of illusion and mystery, shadowed by a fear of the unknown and tinged with anxiety and intuition. It suggests that appearances may be deceiving within your relationship dynamics, indicating a lack of transparency in the situation at hand.
The Sun	This is an exceptionally positive card indicating success, fulfillment and celebration signifying a warm and happy connection.
Judgement	This card signals a moment of crucial choices, enveloped in karmic energy. You stand at a threshold of change, where evolution is inevitable. The outcomes you will experience are directly linked to the effort you've put forth.
The World	The card resonates with vibrant energies of fulfillment, embracing wholeness, and celebrating achievements. It heralds the dawn of a fresh chapter after the closure of the present cycle. In matters of love, it signifies not just success but profound strides towards a fulfilling relationship.

MAJOR ARCANA AND COURT CARDS AS INDIVIDUALS

In tarot readings, court cards and Major Arcana cards not only represent specific energies but can also indicate other individuals involved in the situation. The Pages often signify children or young people up to the age of 16-18, while the Knights typically represent young adults, often under 30 years of age. On the other hand, the Kings and Queens usually indicate adults who are more mature and established in the situation. Each court card carries its own unique energy and personality traits, offering insights into the dynamics and relationships within the reading.

Below offers some clues to piece together the identity of the potential people in your reading by their appearance and demeanour. of the heart.

MAJOR ARCANA CARD	PERSON OR CAREER
Fool	Child or young person, traveller. Careers in social media.
The Magician	A son, brother, adept communicators, and politicians. Careers with a strong communication focus - internet, phones, sales, technicians, teachers, linguists.
The High Priestess	A daughter, sister. Careers in research (librarian, historian, detective), counsellors, psychologists, intuitive workers.
The Empress*	A mother, wife, a maternal woman. Careers that involve creativity such as fashion, beauty, and the arts. Caring professions such as food or hospitality. Can indicate a job where you work from home.

LOVE CHEAT SHEETS

MAJOR ARCANA CARD	PERSON OR CAREER
The Emperor	A father, husband, or paternal man. A prominent businessperson, someone in high authority, government professions/leaders, mentors, or masculine work.
The Hierophant*	A religious/spiritual person. Careers associated with traditional institutions such as churches, schools, and universities. Careers in teaching and advising.
The Lovers*	Twins, business partners, couples. Careers with a one-on-one communication focus, sales, publishing, advertising.
The Chariot	Military persons. Careers in transportation, auditing, networking, and safety.
Strength	Athletes, those that undertake physical activity, working with animals. Careers involving health, dentists, human resources.
The Hermit	Spiritual people, teachers, and trusted advisors. Careers involving writing, editing, data review, telecommunications, computers, teaching, and healing.
Wheel of Fortune	Someone prone to gambling or who has speculative interests. Careers in public speaking, entrepreneurs, restaurants, or investors.
Justice	Legal professionals. Careers in law, justice or compliance, financial institutions, insurance.
The Hanged Man	A unique individual that beats to a different drum! Careers involving the arts, creative writing, innovative thought or businesses, and psychology.

MAJOR ARCANA CARD   PERSON OR CAREER

Death	Careers in the military, financial affairs, insurance broker, drug counsellor, and undertaker.
Temperance	A spiritual person with a calm disposition. Careers in alternative health, civil rights, chef, food, mediator, journalism, or professions involving long-distance travel.
The Devil	People that engage in excessive behaviours. Careers involving IT and business, negotiations, and resource development.
Tower	Hostile individuals. Careers in the military, construction, building, demolition, conflict resolution.
The Star	A female child or young woman. Careers in alternative health or spiritual practice, entertainment, public service, the internet, and technological industries.
The Moon	Mothers or women. Careers involving creative writing, artistry, psychics, veterinarians or working with animals, psychotherapists, detectives, and shift workers.
The Sun	Babies and children. Careers in leadership, working with people, and outdoor vocations.
Judgement	Careers in law, justice, politics, recruitment, and management.
The World	Careers in international affairs or travel, industry resources, teaching, and work overseas.

CUPS

The suit of Cups is astrologically associated with the water signs: Cancer, Scorpio, and Pisces. This suit focuses on emotions, relationships, intuition, and connections with others. Characters from the Cups suit are typically sensitive, empathetic, and deeply in touch with their feelings and the feelings of those around them. They value love, harmony, and the bonds that tie people together.

Physical characteristics often reflect their fluid, emotional nature:

Hair: Ranging from light brown to blonde or even grey, symbolising the varying depths and changes in emotional states.

Eyes: Blue, light, or hazel, mirroring the changing tides of their emotions and their capacity for deep empathy and understanding.

Complexion: Medium or fair, possibly reflecting the introspective and sometimes indoor nature of their pursuits or their sensitivity to the environment and emotions.

Physique: Soft and curvaceous, with a height from short to medium, embodying the nurturing and comforting nature of the Cups personality. Their bodies may reflect their openness to give and receive emotional energy.

KING OF CUPS

The King of Cups embodies maturity, compassion, and the control of one's emotions. He is often seen as a fatherly figure, offering guidance, and understanding. He balances emotional depth with wisdom, showing a serene face to the world. His appearance is one of calm and composed authority, often reflecting a deep inner life and a peaceful demeanour. He suggests a person who has mastered the art of balancing the emotional with the rational, offering support and empathy to those around him.

QUEEN OF CUPS

The Queen of Cups is a figure of deep intuition and emotional intelligence. She radiates warmth, compassion, and a profound understanding of the emotional landscape of herself and others. Her presence is nurturing and motherly, often showing a gentle and receptive posture towards life. Physically, she may appear serene and approachable, with a softness in her eyes that speaks to her depth of feeling and empathy. She represents the pinnacle of emotional awareness, empathy, and intuitive understanding, often acting as a confidant or healer.

WANDS

The suit of Wands is astrologically linked to the fire signs: Aries, Leo, and Sagittarius. Individuals connected with this suit often exhibit the dynamic energy, enthusiasm, and courage associated with these signs. The physical attributes typically associated with the Wands are reflective of their fiery and spirited nature, and might include:

Hair: Dark or reddish tones, often vibrant and possibly inclined to have a natural wave or curl, symbolising their fiery spirit.

Eyes: Bright and lively, ranging from light brown to hazel or even a striking green, mirroring their passionate and energetic nature.

Complexion: Warm or ruddy, indicative of their vitality and constant movement or outdoor tendencies.

Physique: Lean and athletic, medium to tall height, embodying their active and energetic essence.

KING OF WANDS

The King of Wands is a figure of charisma, leadership, and boldness. He typically appears as a mature man, full of confidence and authority. His physical presence is commanding, with a magnetic charm that attracts attention. His eyes sparkle with ambition and determination, and his posture exudes confidence and an adventurous spirit. The King of Wands carries himself with the assurance of someone who is not afraid to take risks and who pursues his goals with relentless passion.

QUEEN OF WANDS

The Queen of Wands is the epitome of warmth, confidence, and determination. She is often portrayed as an attractive and commanding presence, with an aura of self-assurance and independence. Her eyes are expressive and lively, reflecting her optimistic and enthusiastic nature. Physically, she combines grace with strength, her posture radiating confidence and an open-hearted energy. The Queen of Wands is not only vibrant but also welcoming, her demeanour suggesting an individual who is both a leader and a generous host, always ready to inspire and uplift those around her.

PENTACLES

The suit of Pentacles is astrologically associated with the earth signs: Taurus, Virgo, and Capricorn. These signs and their corresponding cards in the Tarot deck emphasise the material aspects of life like wealth, health, and practical matters. The physical attributes generally associated with individuals represented by the Pentacles suit might include:

Hair: Dark to medium in shade, often thick and straight, symbolising their connection to the earth and nature.

Eyes: Deep and grounded, typically brown or dark, reflecting their stability and depth of character.

Complexion: Olive or fair, with a robust and healthy glow, indicative of their association with the physical world and a testament to their dependability and practicality.

Physique: Solid and sturdy, medium to tall, often reflecting their strong connection to the physical and material aspects of life.

KING OF PENTACLES

The King of Pentacles represents a figure of wealth, security, and abundance. He is often portrayed as a mature man who exudes authority and confidence in material and financial matters. His appearance is distinguished and suggests a life of comfort and luxury, possibly signifying his achievements in the material world. The King of Pentacles has a presence that combines the solidity

of his financial standing with the warmth of his generous nature. He is dependable, showing the fruits of his labour through his stable and secure environment.

QUEEN OF PENTACLES

The Queen of Pentacles is a nurturing, practical, and resourceful woman. She often embodies the essence of an earth mother, with a warm and welcoming presence. Her physical appearance may suggest a richness, not just in material wealth but in a life filled with the abundance of home and nature. She might have a comforting and grounded demeanour, with a practical approach to life that reflects her connection to the material world. The Queen of Pentacles radiates a sense of calm and practicality, often being the cornerstone of stability in her environment.

SWORDS

The suit of Swords is astrologically associated with the air signs: Gemini, Libra, and Aquarius. This suit often focuses on mental activity, communication, conflict, and action. Characters from this suit are typically intelligent, and analytical, and may be inclined towards introspection or contemplation. They can be seen as strategic, sometimes critical, and often value clarity and truth. Their physical characteristics are usually reflective of their sharp, mental acuity:

Hair: Light to dark shades, often well-kept or styled in a way that is practical and unobtrusive, symbolising their clear and direct approach to life.

Eyes: Sharp and penetrating, possibly reflecting the keen intellect and perceptive nature of air signs. Their gaze might seem to cut to the heart of matters, indicative of a deep understanding and insightful nature.

Complexion: Clear, possibly fair to medium, suggesting an indoor lifestyle more focused on intellectual pursuits than outdoor activities.

Physique: Slender or lean, embodying their preference for mental agility over physical strength. Their build often reflects their fast-paced, on-the-go lifestyle, with a height that can vary broadly.

KING OF SWORDS

The King of Swords is the archetype of a leader or authority figure who values justice, honesty, and intellectual power. He typically appears as a mature individual, commanding respect through his wisdom and experience. His appearance is dignified, often with a stern or intense look that reflects his ability to make difficult decisions. He embodies the qualities of mental clarity, analytical depth, and ethical standards. The King of Swords suggests a strategic thinker who is not afraid to assert his authority for the greater good.

QUEEN OF SWORDS

The Queen of Swords represents a woman of sharp wit, clear thought, and insightful observation. She often appears as an articulate, perceptive, and sometimes detached individual, reflecting her capacity for unbiased judgment and direct communication. Her physical appearance conveys a sense of elegance and poise, combined with an aura of independence and strong intellectual capabilities. The Queen of Swords symbolises a life shaped by experience, leading to a profound inner strength and the courage to speak her truth. She is often seen as a figure of honesty, insight, and keen intelligence, wielding her understanding like a blade to cut through deception and confusion.

Card Combinations

LOVE TAROT READING WORKSHOP

| THE HIEROPHANT | + | THE LOVERS | Indicates relationship approval and a conventional union, possibly suggesting marriage or a formal commitment. |

In a negative context, it signifies jealousy, anger, or excessive behaviours within the relationship. In a positive light, it may suggest a binding commitment if by surrounding cards.

THE DEVIL + THE LOVERS

THE LOVERS + THE TOWER

Suggests a stressful relationship or the breakdown of a partnership, signifying significant upheaval or sudden change.

CARD COMBINATIONS

Signifies a harmonious beginning, possibly celebrating the birth of something new. When reversed, it may imply the celebration of a birth.

ACE OF WANDS + **FOUR OF WANDS**

ACE OF CUPS + **TWO OF CUPS**

Indicates a strong and fulfilling partnership, an abundance of love, contentment, and satisfaction within the relationship.

Suggests general love and happiness, indicating a flourishing friendship or satisfaction with the relationship or partnership.

TWO OF CUPS + **TEN OF CUPS**

LOVE TAROT READING WORKSHOP

THE LOVERS + **SIX OF WANDS**

Indicates the triumph of love and a rewarding relationship, possibly celebrating the achievement of a successful partnership.

Suggests a partnership experiencing conflict or the potential loss of a relationship due to a disagreement or betrayal.

THE LOVERS + **FIVE OF SWORDS**

TWO OF CUPS + **DEATH**

Indicates major transformations within the relationship, possibly signifying the end of a commitment or the loss of love.

CARD COMBINATIONS

Implies hindrance, restrictions, and obstacles within the relationship, possibly feeling trapped or unable to move forward.

TWO OF CUPS + **EIGHT OF SWORDS**

THE LOVERS + **FIVE OF SWORDS** + **THE DEVIL**

Indicates unpleasant circumstances within the relationship, such as jealousy, conflict, or excessive behaviours leading to a breakdown in the partnership.

LOVE TAROT READING WORKSHOP

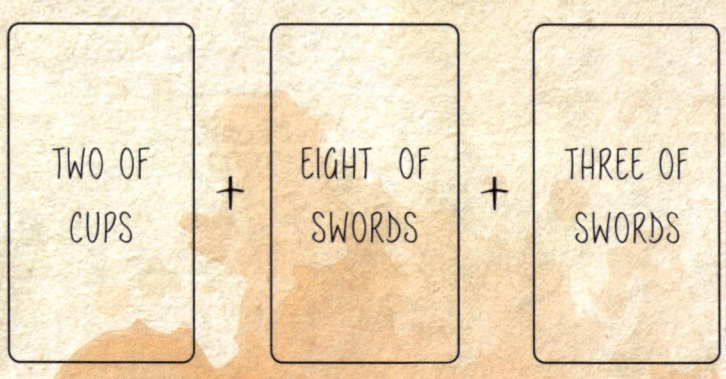

Signifies a relationship constrained by obstacles and hindered by emotional pain and sorrow.

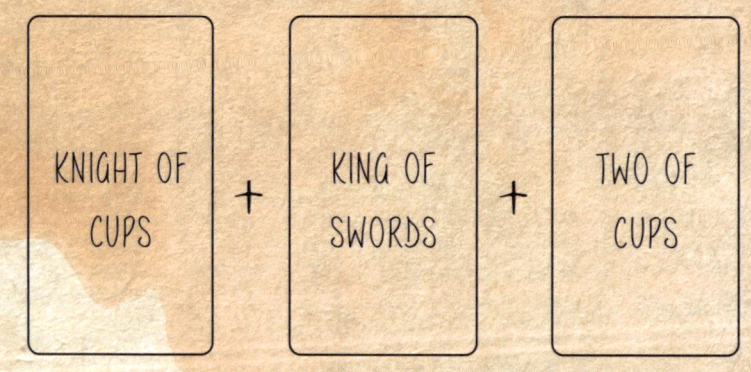

Indicates a romantic connection characterised by emotional depth and intellectual compatibility, possibly leading to a harmonious partnership

CARD COMBINATIONS

Suggests a romantic relationship guided by intuition and emotion, with a stable and authoritative figure playing a significant role

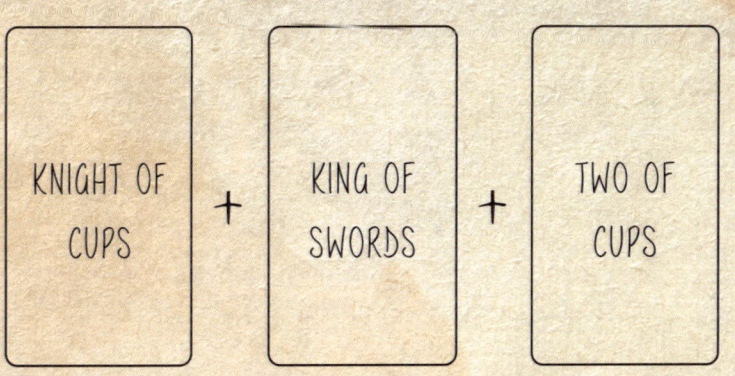

Indicates a romantic connection characterised by emotional depth and intellectual compatibility, possibly leading to a harmonious partnership

LOVE TAROT READING WORKSHOP

| TWO OF CUPS | + | KING OF PENTACLES | + | THE MOON | + | TEN OF WANDS |

Suggests a stable and nurturing relationship with a mature and financially secure partner, yet also indicates hidden fears and burdens that need to be addressed.

| TWO OF CUPS | + | TEN OF WANDS | + | THE TOWER | + | KNIGHT OF SWORDS |

This implies a relationship burdened by challenges and sudden upheaval, possibly leading to conflict or the need for swift action to address difficulties.

CARD COMBINATIONS

Suggests reconciliation or the return of a past relationship, possibly indicating a renewed commitment or the rekindling of love and happiness. Commitment or the rekindling of love and happiness.

CONCLUSION

Well done on finishing this book! It means you're well on the way to becoming an expert tarot reader, specifically in the realm of LOVE! I hope you've found this read as fascinating as it is informative, have a better grasp on the complex interplay of the cards and feel confident to practice your skills and help others unravel their love queries now and into the future. Remember to trust your intuition and embrace the healing power the tarot offers you!

BIBLIOGRAPHY

Chase-Doane, D., & Keyes, K. (1979). How to read tarot cards. Barnes & Noble Books.

Kelly, D. (2003). Tarot card combinations. Red Wheel/Weiser.

Louis, A. (2002). Tarot made simple. Llewellyn Publications.

Kenner, C. (2021). Tarot and astrology. Llewellyn Publications.

Tarot Injie. (n.d.). Tarot card meanings. Retrieved August 25, 2023, from https://www.tarotingie.com

Psychic Revelation. (n.d.). Psychic revelation. Retrieved August 25, 2023, from https://www.psychic-revelation.com

ABOUT THE AUTHOR

A seasoned tarot reader with over two decades of experience, Ruby Jones is dedicated to combining intuitive insights with a warm, empathetic approach. Offering more than just guidance, Ruby provides clarity and deep understanding for those navigating life's challenging moments. Currently, Ruby is channelling years of wisdom into creating an insightful book and a comprehensive course, each designed to share the transformative power of tarot with a wider audience. Passionate about supporting and enlightening individuals, Ruby Jones aims to be a guiding light during times of uncertainty, helping others find their way through the complexities of life.

www.ingramcontent.com/pod-product-compliance
Lightning Source LLC
Chambersburg PA
CBRC091725070526
44585CB00011B/178